GOLF.

LENGTH

AND HOW TO GO FROM 15 TO 5 WITHOUT LYING

Peter Hibbert

First published by Dog Ear Publishing
4010 W. 86th Street, Ste H
Indianapolis, IN 46268
www.dogearpublishing.net

ISBN: 978-145750-292-7

This book is printed on acid-free paper.

Printed in the United States of America

CONTENTS

ACKNOWLEDGEMENTS

I'm a golf nut. I love this game and Lord knows how much time and money I've spent on it.

40 years of golf schools, books and countless lessons. I lived and played St Andrews every day for a year.

So after all this, I got an email from an Aussie friend of mine. Had I heard of John Dunigan? I'm not a religious man but it turned out John was teaching 20 miles from me in the USA. Divine providence? A reward for a well lived life? Who knows, but it led to length, short irons instead of utility clubs to long par 4's, being able to draw an 8 iron (if you are into that kind of thing, but I was) and a handicap drop from 15 to 4 After all those years John showed me in 2 swings what my problem was. So, without John, all my other stuff would be irrelevant. Thanks again John.

INTRODUCTION

Why did I write this book? I'm a chemistry guy and chemistry books are easier to write

Because having played the game for 50+ years, a presumed good athlete, been to golf schools, read all the books, (you never know if the new one may be the one) , I could never get long or 'low'. I never found a golf book that told me how to do it.

Then after all this time I found a couple of principles and rocketed to 170 yard 7 irons, big drives, hitting short irons to previous hybrid wood greens. Low city Nirvana. So I wanted to at least try to pass it on to the huge slug of nut cases in my old position

There are no glossy pictures in this book It's not very long. Parts 1-3 talks about length, who the book is intended for and the importance of turning.

Part 4 is the central point of the book and describes 5 things you have to do, 2 of them dead easy.

Part 5 expounds on the principles if more info interests you at all.

If you think about it, how can you figure out what is important if a book is 400 pages long? An old philosopher finished a long letter by saying "apologies, I didn't have the time to make it shorter" Anyway, you won't care once you learn how to draw an 8 iron

PART 1

LENGTH

This section is up front but an afterthought. After describing how I finally got low I had one last fatal conversation with 270 yard carry son #1. He was describing how one of his students didn't care about going low. All he wanted to do was to hit his tee ball past his buddies   \

Then I realized (duh) that length really is the central point of this book. I do mention it's a different game if you are hitting short irons instead of utility clubs to par 4's . But I didn't emphasise it enough. We all know people who can diddle it down the middle all day and shoot in the 70's, maybe low 70's, but you can't have any kind of rep and go really low if you are short.

Fortunately the steps quickly lead to length. Then the vicious circle is set into motion. Do 5 minutes a day, get longer, can't wait to do a bit more tomorrow.

PART 2

WHY 15 AND 5?

Any Marketing guy will tell you, and I've known a lot, you have to target your audience. This book is for the 15 handicap guys who want to get low. Which means every 15 guy whom I've ever met.

Again, why 15? – if you are 15 or capable of being a 15 it indicates you have some kind of coordination. 5 is just a low number which will satisfy most ams (until they get there). There is a huge gulf of 19th hole bragging rights between a good golfer and a low guy.

Why are three of the steps hard? The steps are only hard because golfers are notoriously pigheaded.

They will pound an incredible number of balls on the range. They will ask you, who is known as a "good golfer," what is your secret? You tell them, they totally ignore you. My hope is that you at least give it a try. If, early on, you are suddenly 60 yards further down the fairway than normal, case closed.

PART 3

TURNING

I was thinking of putting this in the body of the beast. But it really is an important basic principle.

I think it was John Jacobs (the old English guy, not the American one) who I heard it from first. "So often late in the round, when the pressure is really on, people can't hit the last fairway. They yank the tee shot straight left or push it right. It's because they haven't turned"

Watch how many times this happens, even to the best of them, late in tournaments.

As true today as it was 50 years ago.

More recently it's a Nick Faldo mantra – turn your chest. Still terrific advice. If your game starts going bad – TURN. Don't just hang your arms out there.

PART 4

DO 5 EXERCISES OR QUIT THE GAME

Part 4.
Step 1—EASY

Get the right grip for you – grip naturally. See if you have a Sergio left thumb. You wish

An old chestnut. All kinds of books tell you the grip is the foundation of good golf. Sounds good, Gary and Arnold said it but why?

Did they know why? And what did they mean really?

Everybody's hands are different and in my opinion the right grip for you is the one which gives you the biggest wrist break at the top.

How to do it? Let your hands hang down, grab the club with your left, put the right on, turn your shoulders, keep a reasonably straight left arm and feel your wrists break at the top. Look up and look at your break.

Again, the correct grip for you is the one that gives you the biggest break/the maximum angle between the club and your forearm at the top.

The grip will probably be much stronger than you are used to but look carefully how strong the grips of many pros are.

A bit of grip BS which has always interested me and apparently almost nobody else, is how many pros have flexible thumbs that bend back 90* at the knuckle right below the thumbnail. Unless you are willing to break your left thumb to get one like Sergios it won't help your game since you are stuck with what you were born with. A Mr X many years ago (look him up) went into this in much more detail. He pestered all the pros he could find and took pictures of their hands – all had weird thumbs. More of that in Part 6 if you are interested.

Part 4
Step 2—EASY

Get the right stance for you – stand naturally
Revulsion and the men's locker room.
Alignment

Like all of us I've tried and read everything .Right foot perpendicular to the shot line to restrict your hip turn on the backswing. Left foot at 45* to help you release through the hitting area. Yeah , yeah, yeah.

The silliness of all this was brought to me as I was lounging in the sauna of our health club. It is positioned directly opposite to the washbasins. As I looked out at the backsides of 4 or 5 naked guys shaving (not a pleasant sight) it struck me how completely differently they stood. One pin toed, the next both feet perpendicular to the line, the next splayed.

So how can you advise all of them to stand the same? Ridiculous. A much better idea is to stand naturally.

Makes much more sense.

Alignment

Sadly, even if your grip and feet are ok you are still doomed if you don't line up correctly. You have to have your feet and shoulders parallel to the target line. Seems simple but most people stand with their shoulders open which further propels you down the slice road. They grab the club with their left, get lined up, reach across with the right, voila, open shoulders. Put a club across your shoulders, have a buddy line you up but get it somehow. The correct alignment may feel like you are aiming right.

Try to be alert. Even pros, when they go bad often trace it to slipping out of alignment.

Part 4
Step 3—HARD – VERY.

Get everything from your left fingers up much stronger and hopefully get your left forearm noticeably bigger than your right. The Roger Federer/Popeye syndrome.

How? Dedication time. Do 100 left arm divot exercises every day for 2 weeks.

What's a divot exercise?

Go to the bottom of your garden or find a patch of wasteland (may be the same) with an old iron and a few balls.

Press a ball into the grass/dirt half way between your feet

.

Hold the club in your left hand, TURN, TURN, TURN (Step 5) your shoulders fully, feel your wrist break at the top, WAIT, swing down and take a divot in front of the ball..

I'm sure your hand and arm muscles will burn and give out way before 100 but gradually build up.

As time goes on try to keep your head from coming forward as you swing down (see later)

Do it every day for 2 weeks. By this time you may have hit a 170 yard 7 iron so addiction sets in and you will be doing them willingly.

Oh, Roger Federer, – just notice next time you blow by the tennis channel how much bigger his right forearm is than his left.

But, just as we were striding confidently to press I talked to son #1 about this. "But I tell all of my students to hit it as hard as they can with their right hand"

He, probably like many pros have no idea how naturally blessed they are. And what they think is an important swing thought for them probably is disaster for the average player.

I wince when I watch the TV gurus and the damage they inflict on the mind and body of the average player. Just last TV weekend I hear "he can now release his body as hard as he wants" and "he can now fire his hips through". Gawd, I know what they mean but such thoughts, for the average golfer, are guaranteed to encourage an over the top move. Can you image the 1st tee gyrations and future medical expenses?

No wonder students are often hopeless and can't follow instructions. So he's wrong but it did make me think a little more – see Part 5

Part 4
Step 4—HARD – VERY.

Buy a cheap movie camera and learn to swing your hands down on or below the shaft line.
Voyeurism time.

If you are not willing to buy a cheap movie camera and figure out how to watch your swing on TV don't waste your money on this book. All you need is an eBay deal with decent speed so it can stop your swing. Ask your kids how to set it up so you can view and stop your swing on TV.

Break open the camera, shoot yourself from the rear. Tripod helps. Swing. Playback on TV.

Two swings convinced me of the failings of a lifetime.

Shaft line – the line at address from the ball up through the left hand and shaft and continued above the shoulder.

Don't know about the new TV's but you used to be able to draw the shaft line with an erasable pen on the TV. As you swing back you will see the hands starting on the shaft line, going back on it and then as the shoulders turn, will go above it. They have to if you have any kind of shoulder turn.

At the top the hands will be clearly above it. Now, crisis time. As you make the first move down I bet your hands will stray outside the line. You are done for. Over the top. The origin of no power, the banana ball, yank left and other good things.

So, you have to find some kind of swing thought which means something to you which will get your hands on the shaft line immediately you start down.

Forget leg, rear end thoughts.

Swing "back", push your hands back, swing at something 45* back of the target line.

Whatever works.

The correct feeling will probably feel *way* inside and all arms.

You have to check this with a camera

The camera exercise has at least two benefits

You will be amazed to see you don't do what you think you are doing

After an initial period of depression, self esteem will increase - I haven't met a golfer yet who didn't like seeing his/hers golf swing, especially if it's improving.

Part 4
Step 5—HARD – VERY.

Keep your head still while doing 4. The lady pro feeling

Duh, but both Nicklaus and Palmer said this was the key to them getting really good. Who am I but what I think they particularly meant was to keep it still *on the downswing*

And now, after I had written the manuscript, and looked in book after book after book trying to find it, I hear it for the first time on TV by someone reputable. Tom Watson no less. I was flipping through the channels and here he was giving a clinic in Dubai. And he says, paraphrasing, "the most important thing in golf is to keep your head still. My father taught me this when I was 6 years old."
He went on and on about a still spine but the basic point had been made.

Back to the original script - sounds easy but feels very contorted when you get it right. Note how unbelievably still the peaks of pro's caps stay on the downswing. Some go down a little but none of them move forward. Now look at your swing.

This is a big key to distance. You can't hit the ball a long way if you are lurching towards the target thinking of trying to hit it with your right hand, legs, rear end etc.

If you watch the ladies they often seem to drop down on the downswing. This is what it can feel like to stop your head from moving forward.

PART 5

MORE INFO ON THE EXERCISES.

PART 5
STEP 1

The correct grip for you and the dreaded LAG.

Wow, the book is half way done and the LAG hasn't been mentioned. As in Part 5 the best grip is the one that gives you the maximum break at the top.

Why? Because if you are to preserve an angle or lag coming down and get your hands in front of the ball at impact it may be best to get as big a one as possible at the top and before you start down.

Unless of course you can downcock a la Sergio but let's not go there.

There appear to be a few exceptions but almost all pros fully cock their wrists at the top. Look at Lorena Ochoa and Geoff Oglivy. Terrific big 'fists' at the top'

Many thousands of words have been written about this lag or late hit. Many more thousands of useless hours have been spent by ams trying to get there. All to no avail.

You can't watch a golf tournament these days without a slomo sequence of a pro hitting a wedge with his hands ahead of the ball. Books and books written on how important this lag is.

The well worn lag argument just won't go away and has just been resurrected under the guise of modern technology. Now, ultra high speed photography has revealed the "one thing in common/secret" even of all the old time greats. '

Surprise, surprise but this 'one thing in common' is our old friend of the shaft being tilted slightly forward at impact. Or, put another way their hands are ahead of the ball

All this of course assumes that lag is a good thing.

But golf is a perverse sport which attracts perverse characters. My much respected John Dunigan is against gritting your teeth and trying to hold the angle/clubhead back (I think). I remember him demonstrating for me a 'lag' swing – low drive, 230 yards. Then a swing in which he released the clubhead - higher and 50 yards further. Of course he knows much more than I and may teach different 'things' to students of different make up.

He did at least say I was one of his quickest students to get the 'hands on shaft line' thing. But then golfers will tell you anything.

At John's end of the golf knowledge scale (way above mine) is son #1 who is blessed with great length, advocates John's position, just 'lets it go' and hits it hard.

But then, these creatures are blessed (and often supported by their filthy rich country club dads, living through their kids) from birth, Often they can throw 100mph fastballs, 100 yd footballs, have hands like dinner plates and bear no resemblance to the average, even good golfer.

All of this LAG stuff defies science and actual facts which tells us you go from hip to impact in a time which conscious thoughts can't influence anyway. But then again, facts rarely get in the way of golf theories.

So faced with all this high powered advice what does a poor girl do? Yours truly goes with results and video. When I did the 'steps' three things happened.

1. I was WAY further off the tee and hitting 170 yard 7 irons

2. Video showed my hands were ahead of the ball at impact

3. Video showed I was preserving the lag way further into the downswing

As mentioned above, you can't consciously swing down keeping the lag. Not enough time. And your fingers and arms are not strong enough either.

I can only conclude that the Gods were favorable and the steps in this screed, strong arm plus correct angle of attack, produce the long sought after results. Go figure, just be grateful.

It's been mentioned before that pros have a born

flexible left thumb. The thumb seems to be able to be bent back 90* at the knuckle right under the thumb-nail.

Take your thumb and see if you can bend it back 90* at the first knuckle. Chances are you can't. See if you can get a glimpse of pros at the next tournament. You'll have to be quick – the TV boys never point it out. Too busy talking about players short siding themselves and other useful tips. There are many of these distorted thumbs on the tour. As I write Paul Casey is losing to Ian Poulter in the match play championship and the camera just caught his 'double jointed' left thumb.

Whether this helps in setting and retaining a large angle I don't know.

Anyway, if you have one – go play the lottery.

PART 5
STEP 2

The correct stance for you

Pretty much covered earlier. Naked men's rear ends. Disgusting.

PART 5
STEP3

The VERY strong left arm, hand and fingers.

Everything to do with the left arm (assuming you play right handed). Forearm, wrists, fingers. Arnold's hands are nothing short of terrifying and Gary Player didn't do fingertip pushups until he had no feeling in his fingers for nothing.

Rarely mentioned in books and on TV.

This strong left arm theory has elicited the biggest argument with pros. "But I'm rail thin and I carry 270"

Parental response – so can Bubba Watson but there the resemblance between you guys and the average good club player ends

Another small point is that many current touring pros have been essentially that since kids when their country club dads dropped them off at daybreak at the club and collected them at the end of the day. Junior tournaments, College golf teams etc. Not a job in sight.

Not to diminish inherent talents but if you check, many have had a privileged upbringing.

We digress but I suspect the pros don't realize how ridiculously strong their hands, wrists and arms are. The golf swing is a violent act and strength is needed to keep it under control.

And have you noticed how much bigger pro golfers are getting these days?

Don't forget the average pro probably has been swinging a club some 50000-100000 times/year (do the math) since diaperhood. Do we really believe Jack Nicklaus had his wife open the preserve jars?

As mentioned in Part 5, son #1 caused me to rethink the strong left arm. Why why why? 40 years ago I read and buried it too long back there where Henry Cotton said beating a carpet draped over a clothesline with a club held in your left hand was the most important golf exercise you could do. He also hugely advocated strong wrists and forearms against the 'passive hands' theories of the time. But what did he know apart from winning 3 British Opens and retiring to Portugal.

As an aside, from Wikipedia, "Cotton loved the high life, including champagne, caviar and bespoke tailored clothes. He lived for a while in a suite in a 5-star hotel, and later bought an estate complete with butler and full staff, traveling everywhere in a Rolls-Royce.

Years pass. I read where Gary Player advocated a strong left arm. But also what did he know? He reportedly slept in the sand dunes with a cardboard suitcase prior to the 1964 British Open when I had a nice warm bed there.

So the strong left arm somehow lodged in the recesses of my mind but was ignored until I came across Paul Bertholy's teachings in the late 90's. Paul, I'm sure didn't endear himself to most pupils by such recommendations as don't step on a golf course, just do exercises for one year. But I went to his school and his digging divots impressed me. He said you should do them at every opportunity, waiting to tee off etc

But what finally convinced me was my own back yard. Lord knows why, maybe it was a slow day, but I started trying to do 100 every day. After just a week I noticed my drives were getting longer and after two weeks my 7 iron was going 170. So I had to believe Bertholy, Cotton and the others.

But all this strength means nothing if you are not attacking the ball from the right direction. Hence Step 4. How anyone can make any progress without a camera is beyond me.

PART 5
STEP 4

The correct angle of attack and cameras and now Ricky Fowler.

Take my suggestion that your hands need to get on the shaft line (and stay there) immediately you start the downswing. Watch the pros. Easier seen with some rather than others. But when you start looking for the inside move a huge number of them do it. Some like Sergio very noticeably drop the club onto this line. Some obviously don't but they have had a lifetime and more ability than us to manipulate their hands.

The new Sergio, minus his Spanish lady charm, is Ricky Fowler who also seems to be ridiculously inside and it's easy to see.

The problem with 99% of us is that on the backswing our hands start on the shaft line (they have to). As we continue to turn our shoulders the hands are lifted above this line.

Then, at the top, we are going to crush the sucker

You are told "hit it as hard as possible with your right? "rotate your body" "hit it with your rear end/legs"

The worst kind of advice for the average hack. These such "tips" all encourage you not to TURN, (Part 3) , finish the backswing and lunge. The right shoulder comes fractionally around at the start of the downswing, the hands move across the shaft line and you are done.

This slight move is incredibly deceptive; you can't feel it and often will not be convinced even by the camera. Even my athletic son in law, normally a reasonable man, was convinced I had shot his video from the wrong angle.

Armed with our used eBay movie camera you can immediately see this.

It's a depressing feeling to see in 2 swings that you have been re-enforcing a lousy movement all these years on the driving range.

So how do you make the right move?

How do you get your hands on the shaft plane?

You just have to find a feeling that will do this for you and confirm it with the camera

This feeling is incredibly inside, all hands and arms swinging down somewhere at the back of you with nothing else moving.

Forget hitting it with the legs, strong muscles, rear end etc. They are important but not what you should be feeling. You can feel you are pushing your hands back, swinging at the ball washer (yes, THAT far back) a tree, anything really back of you.

And all of this after you have consciously felt your wrists break.

It's easier when practicing. You can put your golf bag 45* backwards of the line of flight and aim at that. Mentally visualize something at the back of you to swing towards. Some people spray paint a figure eight on the grass. Whatever works.

Sooner than you think you will be able to sense where your hands should be. I may be recollecting wrongly but I think Gary Player also said you cant get better until you can feel where your hands are. I didn't understand this either for 40 years.

PART 5
STEP 5

Keep your head still/back coming down

Ha, what could be easier? Strangely, almost no ams do it. When you lurch forward a fraction coming down, your 300 yard bomb is history.

Trust me.

Jack Grout didn't hold Nicklaus' hair day after day for nothing. Palmer also said it took him forever to learn how to keep his head still. And now Tom Watson. Not bad company.

I think they really meant keep your head still on the downswing. Rigidly locking your head going back can constrict the whole swing. Back to the videotape and learn how to keep it still coming down. It's a body wrenching experience often best illustrated by watching lady pro swings.

Watch the peak of the pros caps coming down. They may drop down a little but it's amazing how still they stay relative to the vertical. A point rarely mentioned by the TV experts. Too busy trying to get you to feel where your spine is while swinging.

PART 6.

LAST RAMBLINGS

THE HANDS

As you make some kind of progress on getting a Popeye left arm and getting your hands on the shaft line you may want to start fooling around with your hands.

Trying to manipulate your hands through the hitting area is a conventional no no. Only takes fractions of a sec for them to go from your right hip to the ball etc etc etc.....

But, take a look at pros hands a foot or so past the ball. They have completely turned over.

It's been my experience that once you have the big arm and the shaft line deal you can mess around rotating your hands through the hitting area. That's how you get to draw the 8 iron. If you don't have the strength and angle of attack all hell will break loose if you try to turn your hands over. Get the big forearm and shaft line and see what happens. With me the 170 yard 7 irons and big drives came after about 2 weeks of divot digging and as a big, pleasant surprise. It's all very satisfying

PART 7.

THE MARKETING

Finish as we started – the objective of writing this book. There was one you say?

A problem with golf instruction books and I've read hundreds (we golfers tend to exaggerate but as we speak there are 50+on my bookshelves), is that they try to be all things to all people. Ask any club pro after a few drinks and they will regale you with stories of students who just can't be taught. Hence the generic joke "take 6 lessons and quit"

A basic marketing principle is to target your product. That's what 15-5 is based on.

15 handicap people who are nutty enough to put in at least 2 weeks of repetitive divot digging (only takes 5 mins/day) are the targets of this book.

So, that's about it. Not too difficult really and the joy in being WAY down the fairway, over the hump you could never get to, in places you have never been before really is terrific. Golf is a lot easier when you are hitting short irons in rather than hybrid woods. And think of the ………

Now, once you get to 5 ish the short game nightmare begins. But that's another story.

CPSIA information can be obtained at www.ICGtesting.com
Printed in the USA
243121LV00003B/1/P